The SPORTS HEROES Library

Football's CUNNING COACHES

Nathan Aaseng

Lerner Publications Company • Minneapolis

To Doug, Vicki, Kelli, and Jon

LIBRARY OF CONGRESS CATALOGING IN PUBLICATION DATA

Aaseng, Nathan.
  Football's cunning coaches.

  (The Sports heroes library)
  SUMMARY: Includes biographies of eight professional football coaches: George Halas, Paul Brown, Vince Lombardi, Tom Landry, Don Shula, Bud Grant, George Allen, and Chuck Noll.

  1. Football coaches—United States—Biography—Juvenile literature. [1. Football coaches] I. Title.

  GV939.A1A165   796.332'092'2 [B] [920]   80-29252
  ISBN 0-8225-1065-0

Copyright © 1981 by Lerner Publications Company

All rights reserved. International copyright secured. No part of this book may be reproduced in any form whatsoever without permission in writing from the publisher except for the inclusion of brief quotations in an acknowledged review.

Manufactured in the United States of America
International Standard Book Number: 0-8225-1065-0
Library of Congress Catalog Card Number: 80-29252

2 3 4 5 6 7 8 9 10 90 89 88 87 86 85 84 83 82

Contents

Introduction		5
1	George Halas	9
2	Paul Brown	19
3	Vince Lombardi	27
4	Tom Landry	37
5	Don Shula	47
6	Bud Grant	55
7	George Allen	64
8	Chuck Noll	73

Coach Tom Landry, who has led the Cowboys since 1960, has taken Dallas to the Super Bowl a record five times.

Introduction

How important is a head coach to a football team? After all, it's the guys in the pads and helmets on the field who win the games. The players are the only ones who can actually score points or make tackles. During a game, the coaches stand on the sidelines and do not appear to be contributing much. Some may shout at players and officials and show their joy or disgust with the game. Others watch motionless and look no more excited than if they were watching the hands go around on a clock.

But a football game itself tells little about what a coach does. Long before the first game of the season, the coach is making decisions. The choices he makes will often make the difference between a winning team and a losing team.

One of the coach's most important jobs is to recognize talent. He often has very little time to decide whether or not a player is worth keeping. Once a coach has rounded up the best players he can get, his next task is to teach them. He wants his players to learn all the tricks of playing their positions. Since it is impossible for him to coach all of the 40 players on his team, he hires the best teachers he can find as his assistant coaches.

As the season draws nearer, the coach must make sure his team is prepared for its opponents. Because every team plays the game differently, a coach will want to snoop out what each opponent is likely to try against his team. He wants to make sure his team isn't in for a lot of surprises.

As if he didn't have enough worries, the coach must also make sure his players are working as a team. If players are not doing their jobs or are having problems getting along with their teammates, the coach must do something fast.

And while the playing of the actual game is only a small part of coaching, during the game it is still the coach who makes the final decisions on when to punt, when to try for a touchdown, or when to settle for a field goal.

A coach often has such a strong influence on his

team that the team actually begins to act like the coach. George Halas, for example, was a rough fighter, and his Bears were the same way. The Steelers display the same toughness as their coach, Chuck Noll. Fiery Red Miller coaches a Denver Bronco team that can be just as emotional as he. The list goes on: Tom Landry's precision-drilled Cowboys, Hank Stram's flashy Chiefs of 1970, Bud Grant's cool, unemotional Vikings, and Don Coryell's explosive teams have all taken on the personalities of their coaches.

Being a professional coach is a great honor and a big responsibility, and it can be a terrible way to make a living. Out of 28 teams, there can be only one Super Bowl winner. Yet each coach is expected to win. When a team fails too many times, the coach is held responsible. That alone tells how important football owners consider coaches. The eight coaches included in this book are some of the few who have enjoyed long careers at this risky, rewarding job.

George Halas, shown with players Ray Berry (82) of the Baltimore Colts and Detroit Lion Terry Barr (41), coached the West to a 31-17 victory in the East-West Pro Bowl in 1964.

1
George Halas

No one likes to see a player get hurt. But pro football should be grateful for a baseball injury that occurred back in 1919. That year a tough rookie right fielder, George Halas, broke into the New York Yankees' lineup. Halas seemed well on his way to a successful career until a hard slide into third base injured his hip. He never played well after that, and before the year was over, Halas was out of baseball for good. But this injury would not end Halas' career in sports.

During the following year, 1920, Halas helped to form the National Football League (NFL). His efforts brought the sport of football from a money-losing business to the success it enjoys today. And today, sixty years after the birth of the NFL, Halas is still a top man in football. The Chicago Bears think it would take a really special person to replace Halas. After all, the man who replaced him in the Yankee outfield was named Babe Ruth!

George was born in Chicago, Illinois, in 1895. Like many of his friends, he grew up in a poor family. George's father had immigrated to America from Czechoslovakia and was never able to make much money. From an early age, George and his brothers worked as janitors to help support their family. But George spent whatever spare time he could find on the football or baseball field.

Even though he was a better baseball player, the rough game of football was George's favorite sport. Although small for his age, he proved he was tough enough to play football. In high school, weighing only 140 pounds, he played tackle, and his fierce play soon attracted the attention of college coaches.

After a successful high school career in both baseball and football, Halas played football for the University of Illinois and quickly became a favorite with the fans. He liked to run with the ball, slamming into tacklers at full speed on every occasion. Because he only weighed 170 pounds, the coach was afraid Halas would kill himself. So he hastily switched George to an end position.

After college Halas decided to make a living putting his excellent baseball skills to work and joined the New York Yankees. His career had barely begun, however, when it ended with his hip injury. Once again Halas turned to his favorite sport—football. George was convinced that football was exciting enough to attract crowds. So in 1920, sitting in an automobile showroom, Halas and representatives from 11 different football teams held a meeting and formed the American Professional Football Association, or what is now known as the National Football League.

Halas had the backing of a Decatur, Illinois, businessman, A. E. Staley, the owner of Staley Starchworks. Staley had hired George to run his team, the Decatur Staleys. George quickly collected a top crew of players, and the Staleys lost only one game that first year.

It looked as though the Decatur Staleys were off to a good start. But Staley Starchworks was losing money, so in 1922, after only one year, A. E. Staley decided to drop his football team. He offered the team to Halas, along with $5,000 if Halas would agree to keep the Staley team name for one year.

Halas accepted Staley's offer, moved the team to Chicago, and made halfback Dutch Sternaman his partner. (Sternaman was to remain part owner of the Staleys until Halas bought him out in 1933.) During their first year in Chicago, the Staleys (later to be named the Chicago Bears) finished number one in the NFL.

In spite of the fact that he had been given the number one team in the league, Halas was not sure he had gotten a good deal. The team had no coach, no trainer, and no public relations people. Someone was needed to take care of the football field and to sell tickets. Since the Bears had no money to spend on hiring people, George took on most of these jobs himself—as well as the job of team president and starting end! And to help support himself, he also sold cars. But in spite of his unending tasks, George still found time to take his daily afternoon nap.

No one in pro football worked harder than Halas did to attract fans. George hired such famous college stars as Red Grange and Bronko Nagurski to travel across the country with him. But it still took a long time before the game was accepted. Imagine today's highly paid players standing on street corners passing out advertisements for the games! That was part of a pro player's job in the 1920s. Even President Calvin Coolidge thought the Chicago Bears were a circus act!

After college, both Red Grange and Bronko Nagurski enjoyed successful pro careers with the Chicago Bears. In this 1934 game against the New York Giants, Nagurski is ready to catch a pitchout from teammate Carl Brumbaugh.

But the more the fans saw of the sport, the more they liked it. Eventually money started to come in, and in 1929 George was able to hire a coach for the team. It seemed a terrible stroke of bad luck when that coach quit shortly after joining them. George had no choice but to take control of the team again until he could find another coach. But in spite of everything, in 1932 the Bears captured the league title that had been held by the Green Bay Packers for three straight years.

Halas soon proved to himself that he was a better coach than he expected he would be. He stayed on as coach and went on to a successful career. On at least three occasions, George tried to retire from coaching, but he always came back to bring the Bears another league championship. By the time he retired for good in 1968, Halas had won 326 games. This was more than any other coach in pro history.

Over the years Bear players often had trouble understanding the fighting nature of the gruff old man they called "Papa Bear." Running back Brian Piccolo argued with Halas for weeks before the coach would give him a $500 raise. Yet Halas was generous enough to pay thousands of dollars worth of hospital bills for Piccolo when the runner was ill with cancer.

As a coach, Halas brought important changes to the game of football, and many of his ideas are used by every team in the league today. Halas was the first to use assistant coaches and spotters who watched the game from the pressbox. Halas also introduced the use of films in preparing for games.

George's greatest moment of triumph came about because he was one of the first to scout another team before playing them. In 1940 the Bears lost

Coach Halas in the mid-1930s

the championship game to the Washington Redskins by the score of 7 to 3. The Bears complained bitterly about an official's call that cost them the game. The Redskins just laughed and called the Bears "crybabies." Such an insult made Halas determined to get even. He carefully studied Washington's offensive and defensive plays and designed plays that would work well against the Redskins' formations.

The Bears and the Redskins met again for the championship the following year. The Bears earned their name "Monsters of the Midway" that day. In one of the most shocking scores in football history, they thrashed the Redskins, 73-0!

From their first championship to their most recent one in 1963, the Bears played football the way their coach always had. They were rough, old-fashioned battlers. In the end, though, the Bears fell a little too far behind the times. Halas had trouble understanding that a modern ballplayer was not necessarily the same rough scrapper he was.

In 1968 George finally decided it was time to let younger people manage the team. But Papa Bear was not about to retire from the game he had helped to build. In 1980, at the age of 85, Halas still went to his office to carry out his duties as head of the Chicago Bears. And he was still one of the most respected voices in the league.

People wondered how Halas continued to hold up past the age of 85. He gave some of the credit to daily exercise and some to his daily nap. But he also claimed the work was easier. After all, George now had someone else to sell tickets, to groom the football field, to take care of injuries, to manage the money, to coach, to play end, and to

Papa Bear

talk to the public—and he didn't have to spend any of his time selling cars! Now he could sit back and enjoy watching a game of football. And because of his earlier efforts, millions of Americans can, too.

In 1942 Paul Brown coached the Ohio State Buckeyes to the national championship.

2
Paul Brown

Have you ever wondered how a pro football team could end up with the nickname "the Browns"? In 1946 the Cleveland team was just starting out. At first there was some support for calling the team the Panthers. But when the owners held a contest to let the fans vote for the name they wanted, the fans decided the team should be named after their brilliant head coach, Paul Brown. From that time on, the team has been the Cleveland Browns.

No one else in pro football has a team named after him, but it's likely that no one has deserved it as much as Paul Brown. In nearly 40 years of coaching, Brown has had only one losing season. More importantly, Brown has taught the game of football better than anyone else in the history of the game.

Paul was born in 1908 in Norwalk, Ohio, an area that was one of the centers of pro football. At the age of six, Paul began to follow the sport. When he was about eight, Paul and his family moved to Massillon, Ohio. Massillon was in the *real* heart of football country and was the home of one of the first pro teams, the Massillon Tigers.

Like many of the townspeople of Massillon, Paul got carried away with the game of football. On one occasion, he would not even eat or sleep until his parents let him go to a football camp. His football fever followed him through high school, where he developed into a very smart, but skinny, player.

After high school Paul looked forward to continuing with football and enrolled at Ohio State University. But the University would not let him try out for the team because they thought he was too skinny and would only hurt himself. Brown did not give up but took his 145-pound body across the state to Miami University. There he proved he could play. He soon took over the starting quarterback job.

As soon as he left college, Brown began coaching. He lost only one game in two years at his first post at Severn Prep in Ohio. In 1932 he moved back to Massillon where he built a legend. In one six-year stretch, his high school team won 58 games while losing only 1 and tying 1.

Brown became such a hero in his football-crazy state that in 1941 at the age of 33 he won the head coaching job at Ohio State. The school that had once refused to let him play was now eager to have him coach. For some reason, though, Paul still had a terrible time getting on to the Ohio State playing field. Before his first game, he was turned away from the stadium because he did not have a ticket. He finally had to toss stones at a window to get his players' attention so they could let him in!

Though his team won the Big Ten Conference championship in 1942, Paul's stay at Ohio State was brief. World War II was on, and Brown was commissioned as a naval officer. Active duty for him consisted of coaching a football team at the Great Lakes Naval Training Station in Illinois.

In 1946 a new league, the All-American Football Conference, challenged the National Football League. The Cleveland team of the new league made a wise and popular choice when they named Brown as coach. One of the first things Brown did was to bring in some stars. Remembering the old college rivals who had given Ohio State trouble in the past, Paul quickly recruited some of these players, including star quarterback Otto Graham and Lou "The Toe" Groza, a tackle and placekicker who passed up his final years at Ohio State to join his former coach. He also brought in black stars like guard Bill Willis and thundering fullback Marion Motley, who had been unofficially barred from pro football since the early 1930s.

Before long the other teams found that Paul was too good a coach. The Browns won the league championship so easily year after year that the games became dull to watch. It was partly because of this one-sided competition that the new league failed after four years.

The Cleveland Browns then tried their luck against the National Football League. The older league laughed at the newcomers. They wanted to show the Browns how tough it was to play against *good* teams for a change, but the Browns hardly seemed to notice that they had switched to a new league. In their first year in the league, the Browns made it to the championship game against the Los Angeles Rams. In that game, they fell behind until the final seconds when Lou Groza trotted out to try a field goal. Big Lou did his job, and the Browns were the 1950 NFL champions.

Paul Brown worked hard to bring the Browns to the top. He taught his players to be disciplined and

Cleveland quarterback Otto Graham carries the ball during the Browns' 30-28 victory over the Los Angeles Rams in the 1950 NFL championship.

organized. He believed in long warm-ups to get the body ready to play. He also believed a person with a quick mind made the best football player and felt he could teach the fine points of football only to smart players who could learn quickly.

Brown wanted to make sure he chose the best players in the college draft and tried hard to take the guesswork out of the draft. Paul startled some

23

of the older clubs by bringing pages full of notes to the college draft meeting. Although Brown knew how to pick the best man, he almost outsmarted himself once. When Otto Graham retired, Brown was in desperate need of a new quarterback. There were several good quarterbacks coming out of college that year, and Brown was sure he would be able to draft one. He was shocked when they were all chosen before his club had their turn to select. Angrily, he said he would have to settle for a fullback from Syracuse. That fullback turned out to be Jim Brown, football's greatest runner!

Paul also knew it would take some experimenting to keep his club on top of the league. Once he watched his quarterback and his fullback bump into each other on a handoff. By the time they had gotten untangled, most of the defensive linemen had blown past them, and the fullback was astounded to see a clear path in front of him. Brown decided this might be just the play to work against hard-rushing linemen. The play, called the "draw play," is now used by every team in football. Brown also used a wide-open offense and studied the passing game to see what improvements he could make in it.

Paul Brown kept the Cleveland team winning throughout the 1950s, but a new owner took over the team in 1961. Brown did not get along with him and a year later left the team that was named after him. From 1962 to 1967, Brown was away from football and spent most of his time traveling and playing golf.

In 1967 a new team was added to the American Football League in Cincinnati, Ohio. The Cincinnati people decided to follow the Cleveland team and asked Paul Brown to be their coach. Although Brown was almost 60 years old, Cincinnati still felt that he was ahead of the other coaches. And they were right. In just three years, Paul changed the Cincinnati Bengals from a group of cast-off players to a team that was good enough to win a spot in the American Football Conference play-offs.

Brown coached the Bengals the way he had always coached. He showed quarterback Ken Anderson how to direct the passing attack, but, as usual, he called all of the plays himself. By 1975 Paul felt he had completed his job of building a strong team. He turned the coaching over to others but stayed on as the Bengals' general manager.

In 1981 Paul saw his Bengals have an outstanding 12-4 season and reach the Super Bowl. But although the Bengals roared back in the second half, they could not overcome a big San Francisco lead, and

Coach Paul Brown of the Cincinnati Bengals

the 49ers held on for a 26-21 victory.

With Cincinnati's Super Bowl appearance, the Paul Brown coaching tradition became more famous than ever. Paul taught coaches how to coach and gave some of football's best coaches their start, including Don Shula, Bud Grant, Chuck Noll, Blanton Collier, and Weeb Ewbank. For his lasting influence, Paul Brown will surely be remembered as one of the most important men in football.

3
Vince Lombardi

Green Bay Packer players were fond of saying that Vince Lombardi treated everyone on the team the same—like dogs. The fact that they could say it with a smile showed the unusual respect they had for their coach. The most demanding, critical, emotional pro coach in the land somehow got the best possible effort from his players. Though he won fewer total games than many other coaches, Lombardi is probably the most famous pro football coach ever.

Vince Lombardi was born in 1913. His parents had come to America from Italy and had settled in Brooklyn, New York. The Lombardi home was a strict one, and as the oldest child, Vince gave the orders to the younger children. Vince was in charge, and everybody knew it. In later years, Lombardi was to run his football teams the same way.

From an early age, Vince was known as a fighter with a temper. So it was a surprise to many to learn that in high school Vince was studying to be a priest. But after two years at a Catholic prep school, Lombardi decided the priesthood was not for him, and he transferred to another school. It was at his new school that Lombardi began to do well at football.

After graduating from high school, Lombardi attended Fordham University, where he was an A student as well as a good football player. He was so good at schoolwork that he helped many of his football teammates in their studies. Vince was not a great player, but he earned respect on the football field. While today, at 175 pounds, Vince would be considered too small to even play running back, then at his guard position he held his own against much larger opponents.

In 1937 Lombardi graduated with a business degree and went to work for a finance corporation. As far as he was concerned, his football days were over. But in 1939, a friend talked him into taking a teaching and coaching position at a private high school in Englewood, New Jersey.

Vince certainly earned his salary as a teacher and a coach. Besides coaching several sports, he taught physics, chemistry, and algebra. He believed in hard work and earned a reputation as a tough teacher. Students entering Lombardi's classroom for the first time dreaded it worse than a jail sentence. Among Lombardi's students was his youngest brother, whom Vince also coached on the football team. In 1947 Vince left the school to take the position of freshman football coach at Fordham University. Vince's brother was about to attend that school until he heard who his coach would be!

After two years at Fordham, Lombardi moved on to West Point as an assistant coach for Army. Under the great coach, Earl Blaik, Lombardi learned a tough method of coaching—as if he needed any more lessons in how to discipline!

In 1954 at the age of 41, Vince joined the NFL. He was called to coach the offense for the strong New York Giant team. Lombardi enjoyed having a good time with his players at New York, but his friendliness had its limits. Lombardi's fits of anger accounted for some broken equipment, including film projectors.

Vince's next coaching job was with the Green Bay Packers. In 1958 the Packers had struggled through a horrible season. The next year, when Vince took over the team, the Packers quickly learned that playing football was not going to be a time for relaxing. The training camp was run on "Lombardi time." This meant everyone had to show up for a meeting or practice session 15 minutes *ahead* of time.

Vince was definitely not a quiet, pat-on-the-back coach. He would shout at his players, bawling out everyone from rookies to the top veterans. It was his way of getting players to work hard. When he criticized a player, he wanted that man to be determined to prove him wrong. Lombardi felt it was more important to have players with a will to win than players with great talent.

The coach's methods seemed to work. No other coach has had quite the success Lombardi had in getting players to perform above their abilities. Two of the best examples of this were halfback Paul Hornung and quarterback Bart Starr.

Paul Hornung had been a flashy college football hero at Notre Dame. But until Vince came to Green Bay, Hornung's career had been unimpressive. He had shuffled around in all of the offensive backfield positions without much success. Lombardi kept Hornung at halfback and was constantly after him

Amid the snow and cold of the 1965 NFL championship game in Green Bay, Coach Lombardi explains offensive strategy to quarterback Bart Starr. The Packers won the title by defeating the Browns, 23-12.

to work harder and to pay closer attention. Hornung later admitted it was just what he had needed to become a top scorer in the NFL.

Bart Starr was a different case. He was a mild-mannered type who never showed much ability at the University of Alabama. Lombardi gave him confidence and showed him how to be a leader and a tough competitor. Starr, too, gave his coach all the credit for making him one of the most accurate passers in pro football.

In 1959, his first year as coach, Lombardi led the Packers to a winning season. The Packers won the conference championship the next year and just missed winning a close game in the league championship against the Philadelphia Eagles. The Philadelphia game was the only play-off or championship game Lombardi ever lost. In 1961 the Packers rolled over the New York Giants, 37-0, for the NFL championship. They were also the NFL champions in 1962 and 1965.

In 1966 the National Football League and the American Football League agreed to join forces. They announced that the winners of each league would meet for the first time in a championship game, the Super Bowl. The Packers won the NFL crown again that year, beating Dallas by 34 to 27. The pressure on them to beat the huge Kansas City Chiefs of the American Football League was tremendous. The Packers started slowly in the game, but by the time it was over, they had shown who was the best team in football. Green Bay pulled away to a 35-10 Super Bowl victory.

The following season, the Packers again beat Dallas for the NFL crown and gained the right to defend their Super Bowl title. This time they thrashed the Oakland Raiders by a wide margin, 33-14. By

Offensive lineman Forrest Gregg (left) and Jerry Kramer (right) hoist Coach Lombardi to their shoulders to celebrate Green Bay's victory over Oakland in the 1968 Super Bowl.

now Lombardi had proven he was the best coach around. But at the height of his success, he decided to step down. Ever since he left at the end of the 1967 season, Packer fans have been longing for the good old Lombardi days.

There was really nothing very complicated about the way Lombardi ran his team. Everyone knew the Packers loved to run simple power sweeps.

Coach Lombardi intently watches the action on the field.

Their offensive guards practiced pulling out of the line of scrimmage and leading a runner around one end or the other. Lombardi made them do it time after time until each player could do his job perfectly. After an emotional Lombardi speech, the well-drilled Packers were ready to perform almost superhuman feats.

After a year of sitting out, Vince decided he could not stay away from the challenge of coaching after all. He joined the Washington Redskins in 1969 and quickly built the team from a losing one into a winner.

Lombardi liked to say he never lost, but that sometimes he just ran out of time. For Vince time ran out two weeks before the 1970 season when he died of cancer at the age of 57.

Today Vince Lombardi is still football's most famous coach. He was a man who sought perfection, and did whatever he could to get his players to try for perfection also. When experts remember the awesome power sweeps of Lombardi's Packers, they cannot help but think they were the closest to perfection that anyone has ever come in football.

Coach Landry instructs his players during a workout.

4
Tom Landry

Tom Landry had to hustle for all he was worth when playing defensive back. As a rookie for the New York Giants in 1950, Tom became frustrated by his lack of speed. It seemed to him that he always arrived on the scene a half-step later than he wanted to.

But Tom was not about to give up. He decided that if he could not outrun his opponents, he would outfox them. He sat up nights, watching game films and taking notes. When the Giant coaches began missing their films, they usually traced them to Landry's room.

For a while, Tom's teammates were not sure what he was up to. But when New York's opponents lined up for a play, Landry would quietly tell his teammates what the play would be. Tom was right so much of the time that his teammates thought he had extrasensory powers! It wasn't long before Tom got to know the offenses so well that he became an All-Pro defensive back.

What Landry had actually done was to treat the game of football as a science. He studied formations and drew up charts until he found clues that gave away the offense's plans. It was Landry's computer-like approach to football that helped him to become one of the geniuses of the coaching world. Under his direction, the Dallas Cowboys have been outsmarting teams and winning titles for more than 15 years.

Tom Landry was born in 1924 and grew up in the town of Mission in southern Texas. Mission must have seen its share of dull football games during Landry's high school years. When Tom was a senior fullback, he and his teammates outscored their opponents by over 300 points!

After high school, Landry continued his football career at the University of Texas until it was interrupted by World War II. Tom joined the Air Force and, at the age of 19, flew 30 missions in Europe. On one mission his plane was forced down, but Tom managed to make his way back to safety.

After his war experiences, it was a more serious Tom Landry who reported back for football workouts at the University of Texas. Being older than many of the other players, Landry did not go along with the usual college pranks of his teammates. While playing at fullback and defensive back, he studied hard to get a degree in engineering.

After playing a year in the old All-American Football Conference, Landry joined the New York Giants of the NFL in 1950. Along with his fine plays at defensive back, Tom also punted and returned kicks. But it was his concentrated study of offenses that made him a football expert early in his career.

One time a Giants' coach came up with a new defensive plan. He told his men that the best way to stop the champion Cleveland Browns was to try a new "6-1 defense." With little in the way of explanation, the coach left the room. Tom was able to show the team how the defense worked and why it would be good to use it against the Browns.

Landry became such a defensive wizard that he coached the Giants' defense in 1954 and 1955 while still a player. The following year, he gave up playing and stuck to coaching. With Landry controlling the defense and Vince Lombardi running the offense, New York was in very good hands.

```
  RCB      R S           L S      LCB


  RLB           MLB             LLB


     R E   R T        L T   L E
```

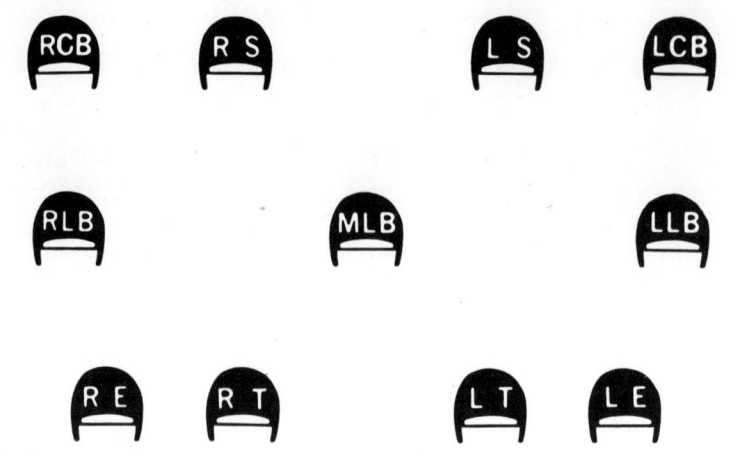

A diagram of Tom Landry's brilliant defensive innovation—the 4-3-4 defense.

During the late 1950s, Landry thought up the biggest breakthrough in the history of pro defenses. He designed the "4-3-4 defense," a defense in which four strong linemen were backed up by agile linebackers. Using this formation, the defense could stop both runs and passes. Shortly after Landry first used the "4-3-4 defense," every team in the league copied it. More than twenty years later, it is still the most common defensive formation in use.

In 1959 Landry wondered whether he should give up coaching and concentrate on his other job as an insurance salesman. At the same time, the newly formed Dallas Cowboys also asked him to be their head coach. Landry decided to accept the coaching job. But if he had known what handicaps he would be working under, he might still be selling insurance. The Cowboys were stocked with three of the worst players from each NFL team and were given no draft choices. Under such conditions, it is not surprising that Dallas did not win one game its first year.

Since he did not have the talent to win, Landry again went to his charts. As the inventor of the "4-3-4 defense," he knew the defense's weaknesses. Before long he came up with a multiple offense to beat his own defensive invention! This new offense used countless shifts of position to confuse defenses before the ball was hiked.

Landry and the Cowboys also put their computers to work to find good players. They designed a complicated system that rated and mapped performances in 160 areas of football play. But the computer could not do everything, and Tom made many of the final decisions about which players to keep and which to let go.

It took a long time, unfortunately, for the Cowboys to show the results of this scientific study. After three years, Tom's coaching record stood at only 13 wins with 38 losses and 2 ties. Dallas fans had begun to grumble about their losing coach. The owners, however, were so impressed with what Tom was doing that, in spite of his record, they gave him a new 10-year contract.

By 1966, 3 years into his contract, Dallas had turned around and was the strongest team in its division. In fact only the famous Green Bay Packers kept them from the NFL championship. The Cowboys battled the Packers in exciting title games in 1966 and 1967 and lost both—the 1966 game, 34 to 27, and the 1967 game, 21 to 17, in the last 20 seconds. In the 1971 Super Bowl, when Dallas lost to the Baltimore Colts, 16 to 13, the loser label was again hung on Landry.

Through all these years, Landry remained calm. On the sidelines, in his neat suit, tie, and hat, he never appeared rattled. His poker face never changed its expression much, and he never yelled at players or at the officials. He believed that the misfortune of losing so many close championships would only help to make his team stronger and more dedicated.

Landry's many years of preparation finally paid off in the 1972 Super Bowl. Landry's Doomsday Defense and solid running attack crushed the Miami Dolphins, 24-3.

After years of play-off frustration, Landry's Cowboys finally won the big game, a 24-3 victory over Miami in the 1972 Super Bowl.

Even after that victory, however, Landry continued to look for new ways to stay on top. One thing he did was drill his team in a new "flex defense." In this defense, his men did not go after the ball carrier but instead patrolled an area of the field. Another trick of Tom's was to bring in the old "shotgun offense" (used briefly by San Francisco in the 1960s) for passing situations. For this play, Tom put his quarterback behind the line like a

43

Tom Landry

punter about to receive a hike. Though it looked unusual and had the experts laughing, this formation gave the passer more time to look for a target.

Because of Landry's inventive coaching, the Cowboys have never had to rebuild. Since 1966 they have made the play-offs every year but one, 1974. They have also been able to replace great players faster than anyone. Before the 1977 season, only four Cowboys remained from the team that had won the Super Bowl in 1972. For most teams, that would have meant disaster. But for the Cowboys it simply meant winning the 1978 Super Bowl by thrashing the Denver Broncos, 27-10.

Although he had been successful, Landry has still received his share of criticism. Some say he takes the fun out of football and makes his players robots who do nothing but carry out orders while he calls all of the plays and assigns everyone his duties. Others say he has no feeling and has no time for athletes who disagree with him.

While all of this criticism bothers Landry, he still insists that a coach cannot let his emotions get in the way. He does not appear excited because he is always thinking two or three plays ahead. Landry would like people to realize that his teams win because they are dedicated to doing the best job they can and not just because of his tricks.

Judging by his record, Tom's method seems to work. His Cowboys have been one of football's most successful teams. They have also been considered a model for all new teams to follow if they want to build themselves into winners.

Dolphin coach Don Shula confers with his field general, quarterback Bob Griese.

5
Don Shula

Donald Francis Shula was born in Painesville, Ohio, in 1932. Like his father, Don was expected to become a hardworking fisherman. He soon discovered, however, that the waves of Lake Erie made him seasick. Fortunately for the sports world, Don decided to give up fishing and to try hard to make a living at football instead.

Shula's firm belief in hard work and discipline nearly cost him his football career. While in high school, Don was forced to miss the opening workouts of his football team because of the measles. Because he felt it was terrible to miss a workout, even with a good excuse, he was too embarrassed to rejoin the team once he was healthy. Finally he was talked into playing and went on to become a fine football player.

After high school, Don played college ball at little-known John Carroll University in Cleveland and quickly became a star player. Shula's excellent play drew the attention of the Cleveland Browns. They decided Don was worth taking a chance on and claimed him on the ninth round of the 1950 college draft.

When he went to Cleveland, Don stood about 5 feet, 11 inches and weighed 200 pounds. Though a fairly slow runner, he was a smart, hard-nosed player. The Browns tried him at defensive back, and Shula responded by becoming the only rookie to make the starting lineup of the Cleveland team.

As a rookie for Cleveland, Don had a reputation as a pest because he was always asking questions. No matter what Coach Paul Brown wanted done, Don wanted to know the reason why. But in this way, he learned more from the great coach than any of his teammates.

In 1953 the Browns sent their question-box defensive back to the Baltimore Colts. Don could hardly feel as though he were singled out since nine other Browns went with him in exchange for five Colts! At Baltimore Shula started at defensive back for four seasons. Because of his knowledge of football, he was known as Baltimore's coach on the field. Usually the middle linebacker is the player who calls defensive signals, but the Colts gave the job to Shula.

Baltimore cut Don before the 1957 season. This started him on a job-hopping tour that took him around the eastern United States. First he was with the Washington Redskins. The following year, 1958, he joined the University of Virginia as an assistant coach. A year later, he took an assistant coaching job with the University of Kentucky. One year later, in 1960, he was with the Detroit Lions. As it turned out, Don was smart to jump around when he did. In each of those spots, the entire coaching staff was fired the year after Shula left!

In 1963 Don finally wound up back in Baltimore. The Colts remembered their brainy defensive back and named him head coach. Baltimore was already a top team when Don took over, and he made sure they stayed that way. In his seven-year stay, Don guided the Colts to 71 wins in 98 games.

But for all of his success, Don's most famous moment was a time of utter failure. In the 1969 Super Bowl, the Colts were expected to thrash the

New York Jets by three touchdowns. Instead, Joe Namath led the Jets to a 16-7 win. It was a terrible blow to Shula, and after the game, he sat staring at the Atlantic Ocean for hours asking himself how it had happened.

Following the 1969 season, Shula moved on to a fresh start at Miami. The Miami Dolphins were a young team, and they needed a strong leader to show them how to play up to their abilities. The players, unfortunately, were all on strike during the exhibition season so Shula had little time to get his club ready for the season.

But when Shula had a job to do, he let nothing stand in his way. To make up for lost time, he ordered the returning players to run four workouts a day! The Dolphins thought they must have heard wrong—no coach had ever before dreamed of four workouts a day.

All the complaining the Dolphins did about Shula stopped when he showed them how his methods would help them win. In his first year, Don improved Miami's record from 3 wins, 10 losses, and 1 tie to 10 wins and 4 losses. The following year the young Dolphins swept through the play-offs to the 1972 Super Bowl. But the Super Bowl again ended in disaster for Don when Miami was pounded by

Part of the "No-Name" defense that led Miami to Super Bowl wins in 1973 and 1974. From left to right: linebacker Bob Matheson, tackle Manny Fernandez, middle linebacker Nick Buoniconti, and end Vern Den Herder.

the Dallas Cowboys, 24-3. Now people were beginning to doubt if Don could win the big one.

But during the 1972 season, Shula erased all doubts about his ability to win important games. Not only did the Dolphins become the first team to go undefeated through 17 games in a season, but their defense stopped Larry Brown and the Washington Redskins to win the 1973 Super Bowl, 14-7.

Shula reached the height of his success at the end

of the 1973 season. The Dolphins ran right over the Oakland Raiders in the play-offs and flattened the Minnesota Vikings, 24-7, in the 1974 Super Bowl. Football fans marveled at Miami's unstoppable running attack, and Coach Shula received a lot of credit for his famous "No-Name" defense. His use of three linemen in certain passing situations was called a stroke of genius.

The only thing that stopped the Dolphins' success in the mid 1970s was the new World Football League. The Dolphins lost several top players, including Larry Csonka and Paul Warfield, to the new league. Again Don rolled up his sleeves and went back to work. Within three years, his rebuilt Dolphins were back on top of their division.

Like most coaches, Shula found himself tested by some of the wilder players on his team. But he knew from his days as a rough and tumble player in the 1950s how to deal with such problems. He controlled his once violent temper and talked out problems face-to-face. All he asked of his players was that they see him first if they had complaints.

Football experts say that Shula is the most organized coach in pro football. That is a trait he learned from Paul Brown. Shula's practices are planned down to the minute. And because of their coach's

Don Shula

careful planning, the Dolphins usually know just what to expect from each of their opponents.

In sports the difference between a winning and losing team can be very small. That is why Shula pays attention to the tiniest detail. Once star fullback Larry Csonka was lining up during a routine practice when Shula started scolding him. The coach claimed that Csonka was out of position and could not hope to get the job done from where he was standing. He then pointed to a spot on the ground where he wanted the fullback to stand. Csonka stared at the spot in disbelief. Shula was pointing to a spot six inches away from where Csonka had lined up.

Such small details might not have been noticed by most coaches. But Shula insisted that his team be prepared down to the last detail. It is such traits that have made Don Shula a four-time winner of *The Sporting News'* Coach of the Year Award.

6
Bud Grant

The man who came down from Canada in 1967 to coach the Minnesota Vikings was a shock to the team's system. The Vikings were used to explosive, hot-tempered coach Norm Van Brocklin. This new man, Bud Grant, made the mild-mannered Tom Landry of the Dallas Cowboys seem like a mad bull. Grant did not say much, and when he did speak, he never raised his voice. On the sidelines, he faced disaster and breathtaking victory without so much as a nod of the head. Soon he was given nicknames like Great Stone Face.

Most of the best coaches seem to have been players who did not have much skill. What they do have, however, is intelligence and determination to play in the pros. But Bud is an exception to the rule.

Not only is he intelligent and determined; he was also one of the most remarkable athletes of his time.

Bud Grant was born in 1927 in Superior, Wisconsin, a town close to the Minnesota border. As a boy, Bud loved nothing better than to hunt and fish. By the time he had reached high school, football had also become one of his favorite sports.

Grant started his sports career by playing fullback at Superior High School. Right after high school, he enlisted in the navy and played for Paul Brown at the Great Lakes Naval Training Station. After watching the team's huge fullback, Marion Motley, in action, Bud decided to switch to another position. From then on, he played end.

Later at the University of Minnesota, Bud played on the great Gopher team of Bernie Bierman. Bud was not necessarily a model football player, and no one accused him of overworking during practice, but he didn't play only football. Bud was also playing two other varsity sports: baseball and basketball.

When Bud graduated from Minnesota, he had trouble deciding which pro sport to play. He ended up by giving both professional football and basketball a try. From 1949 to 1951, Grant played for the Minneapolis Lakers of the National Basketball Association. In 1951 he gave up the sport and joined the Philadelphia Eagles of the NFL. Bud showed the Eagles that they had made a wise choice in making him their first selection in the college draft. In 1952 he caught 56 passes for 997 yards and seven touchdowns. But Grant did not feel the Eagles appreciated him enough so he packed his bags and headed for Canada.

With the Winnipeg Blue Bombers, Bud led the Canadian Football League in pass receiving for three years. Then, in 1957, the Winnipeg coaching job was handed to the 29-year-old receiver. Unlike almost all modern coaches, Bud had no formal training as a coach. In fact he never even thought about coaching until he took the job with Winnipeg.

To all the pro coaches who believed in detailed planning and a complicated approach to coaching, Grant must have seemed like a misfit. Since Bud had no clear plan of how to coach, he just used the trial and error method. When asked his reasons for doing something, he would often reply that it seemed like the right thing to do at the time.

His coaching, however, could not have been quite the guessing game that it seemed. Somehow Grant knew how to form a solid football team. His Blue Bombers won four Grey Cup championships and numerous conference titles during his ten-year stay.

Grant's basic idea was that self-control, discipline, and moderation led to fine performances in any field of work. He believed that if a person learned to control himself, success would soon be automatic. A person would automatically start doing the right things on the football field, and it would be easier for him to concentrate on his job.

By the time the Minnesota Vikings hired Grant in 1967, he was thoroughly convinced that his system would work. When the Vikings told him he could take as many years as he needed to build a winner, Grant said he only needed three. He felt if he could not build a good team in three years, he never would.

Though Bud believed in his system, the Viking players were another story. They were stunned by all of his rules about where they could smoke and what they could eat. They nearly fell over when they saw what the coach had in store for them at one workout. Grant spent a half-hour drilling them on the correct way to stand at attention for the flag ceremony. Before long the players were whistling "Mickey Mouse" behind Bud's back to show what they thought of these childish rules.

Though Minnesota won only three games in 1967, Bud's attitude began to rub off on his players.

Minnesota coach Bud Grant, one of the few NFL head coaches to wear a headset, talks to his players.

They began to see that Bud knew what he was doing. They understood why he did not want them to get too fired up and emotional for games and why he preferred his team to stay on an even keel and to play well every week. Grant had convinced them that by giving a solid performance every week of the football season, they would get the rewards they deserved. This attitude finally worked as Grant had predicted. The Vikings became champions of the NFL in Grant's third year as coach, pounding the Cleveland Browns, 27-7, for the league title in 1969.

Over the years, the Vikings have not had many great games. Nor have they had many poor ones. Game after game, the old, reliable Vikings play good, controlled football. From 1968 to 1980, the Vikings won their divisional title during 11 of the 13 years. That was a record unmatched by any team in the National Conference.

Like the Vikings, Grant, or Old Stone Face, as he is often called, has gained a reputation for being controlled. Television cameras always show him with the same serious expression on his face, no matter how tense the situation. Time after time, Grant has explained that if a person wants to know what is going on in a game, he cannot get carried

All-pro quarterback Fran Tarkenton with Coach Grant

away by screaming at players and officials. Grant believes that emotions can cloud a person's thinking at important times.

Grant's attitude about football games sometimes seems so relaxed that some must wonder if he even cares about the game. Many NFL coaches stay up late at night and get up early the next morning to prepare for a pro game. But Bud is different. One Sunday Bud showed up ten minutes late for

Bud Grant

the team bus. He apologized for being late. He had been fixing his boy's bike and had just lost track of the time!

Although he often seems overly calm during a game, Bud is actually hard at work. He is one of the few head coaches who wears a set of headphones during the game. By listening to his players and his coaches in the pressbox, he has all the facts on hand for making decisions.

Grant is a coach who believes in rewarding players

who have given years of faithful service. He does not cut them from his team until he is absolutely certain they can no longer do the job. As a result, Vikings such as Jim Marshall, Mick Tinglehoff, and Fran Tarkenton were able to play longer than most players of their time.

Bud Grant's main embarrassment has been the Super Bowl. Because of the four straight one-sided losses his teams have suffered in Super Bowl games, people often forget how successful a coach he has been. They complain that he is too even-tempered and that his teams do not have that extra drive it takes to win championships.

Grant, however, does not stay around long enough at the end of the season to listen to such talk. He does not spend winters fretting about the season or plotting ways to win next year. Instead he heads for his cabin in the woods. At the cabin there is no sign of anything having to do with football and only a very brave or a very foolish person dares to bring up the subject. Grant believes that too much of anything is not healthy—including football. Instead he spends his winters relaxing, knowing that he has made the Vikings a pro power for almost two decades.

7
George Allen

A professional coach's job is about as safe as a mouse stealing cheese out of a trap. One false move, and he is finished. If a coach does not win football games, he's fired. If the players do not get along with him, it is the coach who is usually fired. Then there is the strange case of George Allen.

Allen has twice taken over poor teams and turned them into winners almost overnight. He is the only coach with more than 100 pro wins who has *never* had a losing season. He also gets along well with his players. But in spite of his excellent record, Allen has been fired four times in ten years. Obviously George Allen is a *most* unusual coach.

Always spirited, coach George Allen tries to arouse his team.

George was born in Detroit, Michigan, in 1918. He did fairly well in sports as a boy, particularly in football, basketball, and track. But even as a youngster, George had different ideals than most boys. While others dreamed of playing pro ball, George dreamed of coaching.

Allen went to college to help him reach his coaching goal. He attended Eastern Michigan University, Marquette University, Alma College, and the University of Michigan with time in the military service sandwiched in between before he finally began his career.

After receiving his master's degree, Allen took a job at Morningside College in 1949. George did more than coach at the little Iowa school. As a professor, he was also expected to teach a full load of studies. After a few years, George moved on to Whittier College in California. It was the same school that one of his greatest fans, Richard Nixon, had attended. Allen spent six years there in charge of the football team before joining the pro ranks.

Impressed by his record as a college coach, the Chicago Bears hired George to take care of their defense. Within a few years, Allen had formed one of the league's roughest and most feared defensive units. In 1963 that defense brought fame to Allen.

George Allen

Despite a low-scoring offense, the Bears' defense was powerful enough to take the team to the NFL championship game which they won, 14-10. In that game, the Bears completely shut down the New York Giant's star quarterback, Y. A. Tittle, intercepting 5 of his passes.

This powerful defensive performance of Allen's Chicago Bears was still fresh in the minds of the Los Angeles Rams when they needed a new coach in

1965. Eagerly they signed George to a new contract. Allen's head coach at Chicago, George Halas, did not want to see his best coach leave. But after a long legal battle, Halas finally let Allen go.

George had a big job ahead of him. The Los Angeles Rams had fallen on hard times since the days of their two quarterback stars, Bob Waterfield and Norm Van Brocklin. Allen arrived to find a team that had gone seven years without a winning record. He started his job by building a rock-solid defense around the defensive linemen—Merlin Olsen, Roosevelt Grier, Deacon Jones, and Lamar Lundy. This group played so well together that they became known as the "Fearsome Foursome." Again led by the defense, Allen's team became a winner in his first season. Year after year, the Rams were very nearly the top team in football. But, unfortunately, they never did well in the play-offs.

Meanwhile the Rams' owners thought George was getting too much power in running the club and was taking over their jobs. So in 1969 they announced that he was fired. But this action outraged the Rams' players and their fans. Fans called in to say they would not come to the games if Allen was not the coach. And, according to the players, there would not be any games to watch because if

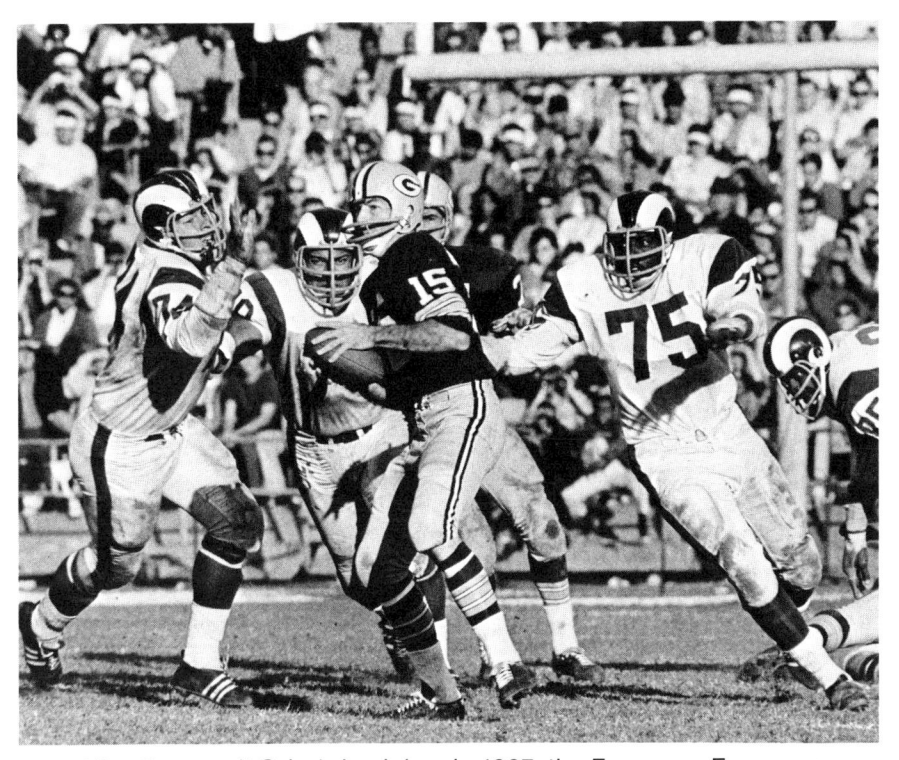

After Roosevelt Grier's leg injury in 1967, the Fearsome Foursome consisted of (left to right) Merlin Olsen, Roger Brown, Deacon Jones, and Lamar Lundy. Here they gang up on Packer Bart Starr.

Allen went, they weren't going to play. The Rams' officials sheepishly backed down and rehired him. But after a frustrating season in which the Rams missed the 1970 play-offs, Allen lost some of his support. This time the Rams were able to get rid of him without such a commotion.

The year Allen was fired was the year the Washington Redskins were looking for a miracle worker. This team's history had been even sorrier

69

than the Rams'. Redskin teams had managed four winning seasons in the last 25 years. The Redskins offered Allen the job as head coach. Allen took the job and told the Redskins that their wait for a good team was over. Many experts thought it would take Allen years of careful drafting and coaching to make Washington a strong team.

Allen did just the opposite of what experts thought he should do. "The future is now," said Allen. He then traded away most of the Redskins' draft choices for the next 10 years! Instead he stocked his team with players that other teams didn't want. Older players such as Ron McDole and Billy Kilmer streamed into camp. Many people thought Allen was crazy trading for players with only a few years left in their careers. They called his team the "Over-the-Hill Gang." When Allen traded for many of his trusted veterans of his former Rams' team, the writers called his team the "Ramskins."

Most professional football coaches are horrified at the thought of "problem" players. These are men who don't seem to have the right attitude to be winners. Allen claimed there was no such thing as a problem player. If you treat a player well, Allen reasoned, he will play well. To prove his point, he traded for "problem" players such as Verlon Biggs and Roy Jefferson. Sure enough, they only gave problems to Redskin opponents.

But the surprises from Allen were not over. He built a half-million dollar training park in Washington, D.C., filled with the best football equipment and surrounded by a fence and guards. It even had two football fields—one with grass and the other with an artificial surface. Allen was happy to give the players whatever they wanted if he could arrange it. He wanted the team to be content so they would worry about nothing but football.

Word spread that Allen was too worked up about football. Unlike most professional coaches, Allen liked to fire up his team. He used emotional speeches, slogans, and all kinds of gimmicks to help him. Critics said that Allen wanted to win so badly that he would spend any amount of money. They thought his great will to win had made him unreasonable, if not hysterical.

But Allen and his "Over-the-Hill Gang" brought their fans instant success, with 9 wins, 4 losses, and 1 tie in Allen's first year. As on every Allen team, a strong defensive unit led the way. In his seven years with the Redskins, the team made the play-offs five times. George came within one game of reaching his lifelong goal of a Super Bowl win, but Miami beat Washington, 14-7, in 1973.

As time went on, the Redskin owners started to wonder about George. The veterans were starting to retire. Where were the Redskins going to get new players? Allen had traded away most of the draft picks. The Redskins finally decided that George's unusual coaching style was too much for them. They let him go after the 1977 season.

As usual there was someone to pick him up. His old team, the Rams, rehired him that year. But after two games in the exhibition season, the Rams' owner stunned the football world by firing Allen. Perhaps he, too, found Allen's unusual way of running things just too uncomfortable.

Regardless of what happens to him in the future, George Allen has been a truly amazing coach. His 12-year record of 116 wins, 47 losses, and 5 ties is one of the best in NFL history. Almost no one believes in his "the future is now" approach to the game, but the fact remains that George Allen has been one of football's most successful coaches.

8
Chuck Noll

More people are learning how to spell the name of the Pittsburgh Steelers' coach these days. For several years, Chuck Noll was confused with Chuck Knox, the former coach of the Los Angeles Rams who now coaches at Buffalo. It was easy to overlook Noll because he never said much or did anything to make the headlines. Instead he spent most of his time glaring at missed blocks and at reporters who asked him questions.

Noll still tries to avoid the spotlight and has found a much quicker way to win respect as a fine coach. He wins Super Bowls. Chuck's Pittsburgh Steelers have been dominating pro football since the mid 1970s and have won a record four Super Bowl games. With a record like that, Chuck Noll must be doing something right.

Charles Henry Noll was born in 1932 in Cleveland, Ohio—in the middle of football country. At an early age, he began to play football. On the high school football field, he was known as a good, solid player who could fill in wherever he was needed. His talent was not tremendous, but he was a smart player and determined to do his job.

After high school, Chuck played football at Dayton University in Ohio. He was the sort of in-between player who coaches have trouble placing in the right position. At just over 200 pounds, he was not the ideal size for a lineman. But he didn't have the quickness that coaches like to see at other positions either. Dayton ended up by using him at both offensive tackle and at linebacker. But no matter what position Chuck played, he tried his hardest. It was this spirit and determination that helped him earn the honor of team captain.

When the 1953 draft came around, Chuck found out what the National Football League thought of in-between players. Noll wasn't selected by the Cleveland Browns until the 21st round of the draft!

Cleveland coach Paul Brown appreciated brains and hard work more than size. So when he saw how well Chuck used his ability, he put him in the lineup as an offensive guard. The guards were especially important to Cleveland's offense because they carried in plays from the bench to the quarterback. After four years as a guard, Noll was switched to linebacker. It must have been comforting for a coach to see him out on the field, knowing he wouldn't have to worry about Noll making any mistakes.

At the age of 27, Chuck decided he had banged heads long enough. He turned in his uniform and decided to try his hand at coaching. Chuck found a job as an assistant coach with the Los Angeles (now San Diego) Chargers. Although he was younger than many of the players, he quickly won the team's respect. The winning ways Chuck had learned at Cleveland followed him to Los Angeles. In his six years there, starting in 1960, the Chargers won five divisional titles.

In 1966 Chuck joined another former student of Paul Brown's, Don Shula, who was coaching the Baltimore Colts. Shula gave Chuck the task of coaching the defensive backs. During Noll's three years with the Colts, most teams found that passing against his defensive backs was a waste of time.

After working in the shadows of Brown and Shula for many years, Noll was ready to lead a team by himself. In 1969 the coaching job at Pittsburgh

Chuck Noll

opened up. The Steelers had been having troubles since 1963. It seemed they were always looking for a new coach and that no one had been able to get much of a performance out of them.

Noll was one person who was not afraid to tell the Steelers' owner just what he thought of the team. He said it would take several years of work to even make the team respectable. The owner was impressed with Noll's honest approach and gave him the job. The recommendation from the successful Don Shula didn't hurt, either.

Noll's prediction turned out to be painfully true. In his first year as coach, the Steelers lost their remaining 13 games after winning the first game of the year. It seemed that Noll would join the long line of coaches whose careers had been ruined by the woeful Steelers. But Chuck was not one to be shaken by a 1-13 season. He continued to patiently teach his young, inexperienced players. He believed it was better to lose for a while with players who were still learning than to trade away draft choices.

Noll and the Steelers started to draft players wisely. In 1969 their first choice was massive defensive tackle Joe Greene. By the end of 1971, the Steelers had also added the rest of their defensive linemen, quarterback Terry Bradshaw and linebacker Jack Ham. These would be the players who would lead the team to the top in a few years.

Chuck was totally honest with his players. He did not believe in having a long list of rules. If a rule could not help a player in his football performance, Noll saw no need for the rule.

Just as Noll had expected, the Steelers slowly toughened into a skilled, hard-hitting unit. Noll taught his men that football is simply a game of hitting. Taking a more active part in the actual workout drills than most coaches, Noll helped to prepare his men to play a rough game. With the help of weight training, the Steelers were soon out-muscling their opponents.

Chuck knows that hitting isn't the only way to win a ballgame. Through the years, he has found several ways to win championships. Pittsburgh's first Super Bowl win in 1975 was won with a crushing defense. In the 1976 Super Bowl, Pittsburgh again won, this time with a combination running and passing attack. Through the mid 1970s, Noll relied on a punishing running game led by Franco Harris and Rocky Bleier. Then in the 1979 and 1980 Super Bowls, it was a wide-open passing attack, featuring Terry Bradshaw and receivers Lynn Swann and John Stallworth, that won the Steelers their third and fourth championships.

Noll's Steelers are famous for their "trap" blocking. In this type of blocking, they let the defensive players go where they want to at the start of the play. Just when the defenders think they are in position to make the tackle, they are usually flattened by a Steeler coming at them from an unexpected direction.

Coach Noll and quarterback Terry Bradshaw have led the Steelers to four Super Bowl championships.

Throughout the losing and winning years, Noll has not always been the most popular coach. He does not believe in being close to his players. He can also be a very demanding person, and even his assistant coaches find he can be a hard man to work for. Reporters also get frustrated by Noll's short answers to many of their questions. But in spite of his ways, Noll has won the respect of almost everyone in football.

Part of Noll's success comes about because he is never satisfied. He often says that his Super Bowl champions have not yet done as well as they are capable of doing. While Pittsburgh fans might enjoy their 1980 Super Bowl win for many months, Noll will not. Chuck's only thoughts are how to do even better the next time.

ACKNOWLEDGMENTS: The photographs are reproduced through the courtesy of: pp. 4, 36, 43 (Russ Russell Photography), 44, Dallas Cowboys; pp. 8, 13, 23, Pro Football Hall of Fame; pp. 15, 17, Chicago Bears; p. 18, Cleveland Browns; p. 26, Cincinnati Bengals; pp. 31, 33, 34, Vernon J. Biever; pp. 46, 51, 53, Miami Dolphins; pp. 59, 61, 62, Minnesota Vikings; pp. 65, 67, 69, Los Angeles Rams; pp. 76, 79, Pittsburgh Steelers.

Cover photograph: Vernon J. Biever